the
dinosaur park

the
dinosaur park

robert minhinnick

For Caryel,

from

Robert Minhinnick
June 1st
'87

POETRY WALES PRESS
1985

POETRY WALES PRESS
56 PARCAU AVENUE, BRIDGEND, MID GLAMORGAN

British Library Cataloguing in Publication Data

Minhinnick, Robert
   The dinosaur park.
   I. Title
   821'.914   PR6063.14/

ISBN 0-907476-48-1

Cover Design: Cloud Nine

*The publisher acknowledges the financial assistance of the
Welsh Arts Council.*

Typeset in 11 pt Palatino
by Afal, Cardiff
Printed by
Antony Rowe Ltd., Chippenham

Contents

Acknowledgements

Some of these poems have appeared or are due to appear in the *Anglo-Welsh Review, Argo, Maximum Load, New Wales, Outposts, Poetry Wales, Spectrum* and *2 Plus 2.*

The Dinosaur Park

Padlocked, green-white, the villas
Glint like bone in the dusk.
The road a dead-end but here's a path
Snaking between houses to a public
Garden. Its lawn's a rug of frost
Behind chainlink where crocuses
Have pushed through stems, white as
Cigarette-papers, the knifepoints
Of their colours: the cold meths-blue
Of steel, a fringe of darker blue.
The path moves on by turnstiles
And a locked kiosk, a bowls-sward
And the asphalt tennis courts.
It winds around the dinosaur park.

Off-season and it's shut. I bend a wire
And trespass over frost that shines
Like candlewax. Hummocks and trees,
And then the other trespassers,
Bolted on to sandy plinths,
Moored in the wrong time.
Out of the fantastic past they loom,
Great engines seized, the inert
Mechanics of some botched experiment.
Absurd, abject, the dinosaurs
Are the unimaginable fact.
I pace their world of huge pretence,
The museum quiet grown around the town.
And yet, what's real, as real as these
Vast creatures poised about the park?
The olive plastic of their skin

Under its icy lamination
Is dimpled like golfballs, their
Footprints shallow concrete moulds
Of birdbaths, ashtrays, litter-traps,
The eyeballs livid as traffic-lights.

History too must have its joke.
They're cartoons come to almost-life,
The dinosaurs, or might belong
To some children's crackling screen.
I've passed the park a score of times
But never glimpsed in its entanglement
These postures struck of combat,
Rage, the slow acknowledging of pain.
And strange to think such creatures shared
The common factors of our lives,
Hurt and hunger, fear of death,
The gradual discovery of betrayal.
But prey and predator are one
And are swallowed up by the omnivorous dark,
The watched, the watcher, and the mammoth's dazzling
                                              scythes.

Now level with the dinosaurs
The path runs on, there's no way back,
As shadows make their imperceptible surge.

On the Llyn Fawr Hoard in the National Museum of Wales

(for Martin Reed)

The fish slide through the lake's cool grip
As the buttresses of Craig y Llyn
Throw shadows on the water,
The orange quilts of spruce dust underfoot.
Piece by piece the hoard is recovered:
Iron black and twisted as fernroots,
Cauldrons spilling their memorials
To ancient sunlight, millenia of seeds,
The pollen of two thousand buried springs
Emerging from the dark throat of Llyn Fawr.

Redeemed from that cold lakewater
They lie in white electric pools;
This spearhead's mottling leaf colour,
Its shaft missing, lake-eaten,
Sickles like the beaks of swans
Worked in inextinguishable
Bronze light, a sword's metal
Burned charcoal-black, the pattern
Of erosion delicate as lace.

Presented here no small sophistication
Of the metalworker's art, that art's
Acknowledgement of something greater than itself —
The cauldron's firm belly of bronze
Yellow as roof-moss, triumphant sphere,
The pin-bolts, brooches, weaponry
Offered to the waters of the lake
In sure sacrifice, their molten substance
Pouring outside the cold cast of time.

Yet saved, they are safe, as remarkable
Only as the tools in my own household.
Behind the glass they are as young as I,
The glass that returns my own scrutiny.
History is not this gear of bronze,
Its patina teal-green;
Rather, it is how it was used,
The association of metal and mind.

The Saltings

1

The men in singlets, dark as Basques,
The women grizzled wands.

The grass is sparse, a few thistles
Where she sits down in front of the flats,

Fingering the globe of her belly,
The man's name needled on her arm.

2

When you are born dumb
There are only gestures to make.

Tattoos are badges of contempt,
A small defiance allowed here

Like the bottle smashed against the kerb,
The explosion of paint in the stairwell.

3

She is standing on the balcony
And her skin is white as heroin.

A child is pressed under her heart,
Curled up like a fossil there.

This is the life that persists beyond our thought
And has no-one to speak for it.

The Coast

By single grains it slowly filled their lives.
Everything that stood against it
Was covered by the thin gold web of sand.

Under the door its drifting gauze, and through
The barley. Along shelves and into the privy
Rushed sand, ceaseless and mercurial.

A teeming of aphids over the leaves,
The passing of a whisper at the door
Was sand, building against useless iron.

Now out of the dune comes the remnant of that life.
A needle's eye packed with golden silt
And a polished edge of broken pottery.

Down a hundred feet, or one, the fields
Are ready for the plough. The plastics lie
Not quite as deep, are dimly mauve and cream

Like winter bulbs. Our ground is blurring,
Losing its angles, but the brand-names push
Out of the sand their familiar epitaphs,

And a shattered bottle reassures that our claim
Was made. Here a tidy rank of caravans
Floats axle-deep upon the creeping tide.

Natural History

I

The glass of the conservatory
Lies like rainwater in the dust:
The vines are wrinkled nubs that never bloom.

Memory shuffles the landscapes
But yours is no random view. Brutally
You slice away the present tense

As if it was something hardly worth concern:
Time's surgeon still who probes a life,
The ribs of moss that crease a family vault.

II

In the workhouse they are knocking down
The black chainlink of cockroaches
Behind the plaster, firing mattresses.
Ticks on the bedding like buttons on a shirt.

The families paying rent on pit houses,
The old men packed like fossils into
Galleries of coal, the laundry-girls and labourers,
Know their lives as part of the estate,

Their natural history, even as they crowd
Along touchlines, cluster behind the posts.
Noon's desperate festival under the Bass
Sign's red triangle and then the game.

III

In the hothouses a long
Equatorial summer.
Fleece on the peachskins
A warm fog, the scent
Of orange leaves sharp
From a nurseryman's cuff.

Waterfalls, and the current's
Bludgeoning carp, a sundial's
Spearpoint flashing at the lawn.
No hurrying there, no human speech:
Only the instruction of silence
On how a man might live,

Watching the grebe-chicks raise
The barest tumult in the lake,
Bobbing under its sheen to emerge
Silvered, their beaks like nibs.
Such secrets there your patience saw
Revealed. And you, their guardian.

IV

Saturday morning overtime's unpaid, and it's
A race to get the crop sorted and washed.
One by one the bunches are pulled down, swinging
Like bells in your hands, the flesh starting to break:
Grapes with the gloss already wiped from the fruit,
Their skins' lustre a drab smoke under glass.

You cut the lawns and trimmed the vinery
For sixteen years. A socialist who touched his cap
And knew the way things worked. And when you passed
The vicarage, always delivered
The newspaper, politely, to the Reverend
Protheroe. Though not today. Today the work leaves

A hot weal in the wrist, the vines' itch in your hair.
And the warmth of the air spells one o'clock.
Over the hedge goes the newspaper
To lie slowly uncurling on the vicarage lawn.
Back page a match forecast, one name in the lists:
The crowd already stamping to the field.

V

Behind the pitch the workhouse windows show
Childrens' faces as grey paper rosettes,
Mothers in the porches tamping a wash,
And distantly, their kneeling men, barebacked
Or in singlets, plucking at the stubborn
Fumitory, squinting at the game.

Sometimes a ball is launched into the sun
But often seems a leech against one man's
Quartered shirt, who gathers it so frequently
And holds so hard, his skin is like brickdust,
Red and darkening. But grassed, finally submerged,
He gives it up despairingly, a part of himself.

And lies there, hair outflung like the grebe mother's
Fine crest. While the lake deepens and the sundial's
Javelin of shadow travels over the pitch.
This time it's the left knee's hurt, two inches
Taller and there might have been a cap.
Under his cheek the yellow earth cracks like pottery.

VI

The blows fall harmlessly against your back
But fingernails leave an etching of blood
On neck and arm, a man's spittle exploding
Palely as grapejuice. Then a newspaper
Waves like a dirty clout in your face.

He had waited until you came limping home
Nursing a stud-scar, luxuriously
Lightheaded after the game's climax,
His whole mind simplified by rage
And astonished indignation at your

Assault on order, the challenge to his world:
A man in a tight celluloid collar
Browning with sweat. You might have stifled those shrill
                                        oaths,
But Councillor, the Reverend Protheroe,
Knew the way things worked. You took a street thrashing.

VII

Eyes narrow to chisel tips.
Sixty years too late you're squaring up.
And it's not the story troubles now

But irony's exotic sprawl
Around a simple fact, the context
Time has built around a life.

Across the road the squat brickwork
Has a pugnacious gleam.
The lights go on in Protheroe Avenue.

A Celtic Grave

1

It's a building site and the tanned labourers
Sprawl on their spades, boots and hair
Grey with the region's topsoil, a pale cement.

2

A man looks down the sights of a theodolite.
Surveyor, architect, he views exact
Configurations, the extent of possibilities.
To him the fields are spread like sheet music.

What's here for me but chicory's
Blue lacing of the chalk, the grey
Mace-headed onions fat with seed?
This way of looking I have
Is a careless navigation of the world,
A track of vision falling now
To an infinity of beechtrees,
The shade where the graves lie
Under crackling mast, strange tors,
Hummocks of land where beechbark's
Olive skin glistens like a snake.

3

We come across a field that shows
Its momentary dew on stubble sharp as syringes.
Trenches run straight and form deep squares
As though they would hold cable or the bronze pots of a
                                                    drain.
And we stay a while sharing water,
The village wine so new it parches the mouth.

There's nothing but our own sweat's evidence
Lying in this ground, and the brittle flints
About us knew only the worm's empire.
Whoever else broke the region's soil
Is robbed of even the bone's substance.

But a silent woman smiles and shows this spoil:
Five bracelets in five plastic bags,
A bronze that rocksalt could encrust
But not erase. Green as cistern iron
They lie like tokens of our own domestic world.
An exchange is made. Three thousand years
For these ordinary hoops, a girl's
Thin bangles left out in the dew.

That child dances invisibly.
I think of her wrist shining, its shaken music.

Big Pit, Blaenafon

Coalfaces dividing like a star.
Our eyes' quick sweep to left and right
As down some supermarket aisle.

Under the rock a museum of work
And death; their illusions of dignity.
We see what we should never have believed.

And forbidden, out of bounds, the other shafts
Sealed off with their gas and broken track,
The fossil-gleam, in darkness, of our history.

Dock

Greek and Irish, the shy Somalian
Make common language the city's nasal whine;
Brothers on the wharf as the cargoes
Come swinging overhead: oranges,
Iron, feldspar, grain, out of the sky
The world's tangible gift, a pittance now
As a shadow shift works the freighters,
Alexandra Dock reproachful with echoes
And this south part of the city an empty hold.

In the chart shop maps like dust sheets hang
From drawing boards, and a last technician
Traces blue fathom lines, as delicate
As webs, the irregular shelving
Of a coast eight thousand miles away.
His pen unlocks the sea. It roars in my head.
The compasses stride a continent
From the white edge of its desert coast
To the equatorial heart; a vessel
Manoeuvres into green Bahia,
Its cabins a dizzying fug of languages.

Walking the dock I find that world
Has vanished like a ship's brief wake.
Across the road the seaman's mission
Is a sour honeycomb of rooms,
The walls of dormitories marbled by the damp.
But where the money came ashore
The banks are moored, ornate as galleons,
All dark Victorian mortar
And the sudden frosts of engraved glass,

Their sooted corbels thrusting like
The jaws of Exchange millionaires.
Straight down to the water's edge
The road runs like a keel.

Eelers

Around the wrecks the congers weave
Their convoluted shapes through decks and cabins,
The sea-invaded rooms of unmarked ships.

Oozing, mottled like orchids,
They are appetite in a sheath of muscle,
Ragged as sleeves pulled inside out.

So ceaseless eels haunt colliers and smacks,
The silt-encrusted cargoes of the sea bottom
Until they take the barb, the reel's arrow.

Then each gill is a flower, a pulse amongst
The wounds. Jack-knives and lump-hammers
The eelers' armoury, gaffs and shovels

Rise against the instinct of their rage.
And the mouths of eels twist like the mouths of dogs,
Their bodies are branches, bits of hose

Beneath the oilskin of the conger fishermen.
I've seen these crowd the greasy flags
Of harbours when a motor-launch comes in:

Men high-booted, zipped against the wind,
Their catch preserved in melting ice — mackerels'
Blue tortoiseshell like fishermens' tattoos

A sudden drift of bodies over the dock,
And the congers hung on chains, ferociously torn,
Their mouths agape like beaten, senile men.

The Resort

1. Surfers

September evenings they are here after work,
The light banished from the sky behind,
An industrial sunset oiling the sea.
I watch them emerge from the last wave,
Young men and girls grinning like dolphins
In their rubbers, surf-riders swept
Suddenly onto this table of dark sand
And thrift, the coastline's low moraine.

And back again to the conflict with water,
Wiping salt-stiffened hair from their eyes,
The flimsy boards pitching like driftwood
On the swell, flattening with the ebb.
Theirs, briefly, is a perilous excitement
When the current lifts them high
And they stand erect on roofs of water,
Balanced on the summit of a wave.

And there they glide, untouchable,
The moment of flight and their bodies'
Instinctive mastery lasting until
They are somersaulted into the foam
And they creep to shore exhausted,
Barefoot, wincing with the discriminate
Steps of thieves, aware perhaps
Of something they might have won, or stolen.

2. Snaps

After the rain the small rockpools
Glitter like a switchboard.
The girls wait by the photobooth
Until the card of snaps slides down the shute.
Impossible, they clutch themselves
And stagger, hurt with laughter
In a wild circle. All strangers these,
For whose face matches the idea of self,
That coveted identity, closed like a locket,
The first secret? They've snarled and pouted,
Hid themselves behind the mask of the absurd.
The images come glossy, wet,
Like something born.

3. At 'The Knights'

I walk into the bar and see the faces,
Ugly, staring, full of youth's conceit:
I don't look round because they're all hard cases,
But take my order to a corner seat.

Swastikas carved on motorcycle leathers,
The empty cider cans buckled in half,
But L.O.V.E. across the knuckles in blue letters
Admits the joke, the world's ironic laugh.

4. 'The Kingdom of Evil'

Afraid of the dark, of being alone,
We come here to investigate
The cause of our unease, the root of a fear
That's a common bond; our inheritance.

Heads torn from bodies, limbs with the pale
Glimmer of fungi; and under glass
A simple and ingenious device
For causing as much possible pain

To a human being. The technology
Is plausible but the terror lies elsewhere.
Here are young men with pushchairs, their giggling
Teenaged wives in wild mascara, tight denim,

And the imperturbable middle-aged
Looking in different directions.
The commentary has a neutral tone,
The history of torture like the history of art,

Periods, schools, the great virtuosi
Of the craft. The henbane Doctor Crippen used
Is a quiver of plastic leaves,
The Yorkshire Ripper wears a tuxedo.

At the exit sunlight slaps the face
And all the smirking children wander off
Into the fair. Behind us, in a darkened room,
The tracery of wax restores
A gleaming tear, the psychopathic grin.

5. The Arcade

The crowd tight-lipped, the cries from a machine;
Slots and levers and the engrossing screen

Filled with diagonals, science's straight lines
And the faint reflection of the player's face,

A serious child cocooned in concentration
As an army reassembles at his touch.

Time is banished here. An age might pass
Before he makes his first uncertain move

And turns away to look down the arcade's
Hundred panels of flickering glass

And the figures hunched like snipers at the dials.
His score of leaping zeros glows in green.

6. On the Sands

Our bodies blur behind the glass of heat,
Sand's unstable element underfoot.
At every breath the same discovery
Of white sea-rocket waving on the dune
And jellyfish like crystal bowls in which
A dark life rots. Who else can know of this?

Slowly as oil the Cynffig slides towards
The sea — a grey treetrunk preserved in salt,
A furlong of bleached rope. And no-one
But us out on the sands, the very tip of Wales.
That shell-sound is the motorway, and from
The steelmill's broken plot an orchid's coral spike.

There is a here and now and nothing else,
The present sucks us in. For the first time
I can look around and find a place so strange
Nothing balances it; there is no context.
Yet death and beauty find a fusion where
The dune halts like a burning glacier.

Our culture has its midden on the sands.
The bottles lie around the beach like empty
Chrysalids, sea-holly holds the strewn plastics
In a green pincer. So we embrace our time,
And in ones and twos the people tread the shore
Gazing about them, each with a question.

The Tack Room

The window is a ribbed green pane
Bubbled like a spirit-level,
The padlocked door leaning on its hinge.
This light, as ever, proves impractical,
A bulb's blind eye swinging on a flex.
It's touch, not sight, that makes discovery.

His room describes another way
Of life, a different point of view.
Uncalloused hands find only
Hostility in its warped boards,
A screen of canvas sacks; the weather-
Blemished iron of mattock and hoe.

Even his work coat laid aside
Chafes an unfamiliar skin.
There's nothing I have the right to take away.
These nails, cold hundreds, in regiments
Of size, the paint that slaps beneath
Its milky scab, whetstone and file,

The oiled immaculate body
Of the vice, all these remain
Unclaimable and unpossessed;
I could not call them mine.
Instead it is fragrance I take
From here in packets of marjoram

And thyme, and a memory
That ignites an odour between
Forefinger and thumb. The room

Is his, the tack, the bitter chives
Whose stems he sucked smiling
Silently, and the orange twine

That measured out the drills.
Pressed into earth such fruits
Are time's deceivers, their
Perennial green erection
Like the flourish of his signature.
The seeds stick cold and sharp against my palm.

The Attic

The ceiling shows the yellow stains
Where snow blew into the attic,
A paper-thin pale moss upon the beams
Wetting my hands as I swing
My weight in through the trap-door.

That frontier crossed, I take to trespassing.
The attic room a pelt of dark, the house's
Dreamless skull. I pause and listen,
Crouched sprinter-like over the boards.
And slowly there identify
The architecture of the drifts,
Their frozen combs of snow a yard high.

The torchbeam's dirty stripe of light
Lies brutal as a scar; no snow falls,
For these pillars have erupted
Like fungi, the midden in the middle
Of the floor a sheet draped on a chair.

In the room below my daughter fights
With sleep, her breath a handsaw's icy rasp;
Above, the aerial's hollow stem
Scraping its bracket. Panic has a metal taste.
Everywhere the mercury-coloured pools
Of settling snow lap against the joists,
And here beneath a broken slate
A drift of lilies grows taller by pale atoms.

I cannot touch this profligate:
The snow is furtive and obscene,
And when the wind rises the attic fills

With particles of light, a television
Screen that sucks me in. The blizzard
Is in the house, its voice like pigeons,
Such soft insistence on its mastery.

And I find I have always lived elsewhere,
That I have never known this place:
Old clothes and broken furniture, a bath
Of bulbs with tendrils black as candlewicks,
Sparkless but for snow. I breathe and hear
A breath returned, the flutter as
My daughter's voice thaws and freezes,
Freezes, thaws, and streetlight falls
Out of the roof like flakes of orange rust.

The drifts are grey and tiered like hives,
The swarming snowpoints hover and subside.
Ice on my clothes is fine as insect-wings.

Images from Criesbach

There is a geometry of vineyards,
Of the dark parallel rides
Predictable as tramlines
Dissecting each hill.

Lost, we ease down, content
To stretch for the silvery
Blush of the grape clusters,
The cold ornaments of fruit.

Light swings like a pendulum,
Then falls out of the sky;
A raiment of metal sheered off,
A scattering of white swarf.

The meteorites burst as regularly
As a pulse, discs of light
On some computer screen,
A night's passage, trailing a glow.

As silverfish across the pantry's stone
Flash towards the companionable dark.

Picking

We break the webs of morning as we climb,
Plimsolls quickly blackened in the dew.
Higher, stooped and creeping now, laborious
As swimmers sucked into the wave:
Then the mist thins out and as we turn
Forty miles of coast swings like a scythe.

Roofs and bridges, a farmyard's sharp silo,
The gas tanks squat as drums across the plain,
And in the west above the furnaces
A tapestry of smokes disintegrating
Like cirrus. But smoking in our hands
Are green-scaled puffballs meshed in webs,
The goldfish-coloured discs of the chantrelle.

We sip the earth. Beneath this mist
Elusive shoals of fungi in the fields'
Aquarium, their silent rage of growth.
We're richer by the weight of plastic bags
That strain to hold the golfball-dimpled
Mushrooms' packed cartridges of spore,
Their skins on ours as cool as porcelain.

The town's a web of tight estates,
And then the guttural street. We tip a field's
Gleaning into newspaper, crumbs and dirt,
The white pestles heaped in a pyramid,
All foetal shapes and icy embryos.
Out of this bag the sting of light,
The tastes that we must labour to relearn.

Orchids

At my foot the pheasant goes up,
Green head twisting like a periscope,
The clatter of its voice shaking the air.

I pass the campfires in the dunes
And find the buckled cans, the spires
Of dying orchids starting to tip
To horizontal in the postures of decay.

The chalkdust settles down upon a corpse.
Its belly is a wrinkled sleeve,
Bluebottles busy as eyes inside that gloom;
The orchids are the colour of its blood.

Secretive, incestuous,
Theirs is the kind of family that wants nothing of the world.
Talented, they ignore the rules.

In our midst they form
A colony apart. They have a different
Use for knowledge.
A different knowledge.

Even in the litmus tints burning in the chalk
The orchids are a cool abstraction of colour.
Approach, and they grow increasingly remote;
Touch and they perish.

It's death that gathers them.
Smugly a secret sinks
Back into the earth.

Born on the M.4.

1

As the light fails
These things remain:
In the mansion house
The silence of a museum,
   Walls of skulls and antlers,
A pattern of bones like dirty drinking straws:
   Darknesses filed away.
In the mansion house
The bottled foeti,
   Eyes locked slots,
   Flesh tinted sulphurously
As the smoke ribbon over the breast.
   Behind its glass the hawk's plumage
   Is a yard of crumpled silk.

2

Nine minutes down the motorway
Is the common I used to walk:
Swabs of cottongrass and the flagon-brown
Sinks of peatwater with their fingerprints of scum.

I pass more quickly now and the car's exhaust
Settles over the ant-thrones,
Green velvet tors a foot high
Raised across the heath, the dew-pits
Where eels tangle like hanks of wet knitting.

But as the wipers swing I'm vanishing,
Headlights drilling into a black wall,
Part of the volley of locked
Unimaginable lives all day all
Night pouring over the village.
Such movement is the illusion of freedom
Yet I've never driven so fast.
On the dashboard time is sealed in its green dial.

3

Back and forth
The traffic's pendulum
Measuring the day.

But always at noon
A ruddy crucifix
Suspended above us
Mocking our speed.
The hawk's parish.

Back and forth
The blind migrations
Shaking the grass.

4

Moonlight gives an X-ray of the scene:
    Under the motorway
A forest of concrete trunks.
White boughs, dark skin.
    The lovers suck
                and probe,
Pulling the heat out of each other,
Discovering the coolnesses.
The black mouths of their bodies open
    Sticky as buds.
Traffic is in their blood,
The exhaust's blue nimbus
Writhing at their heads.
Under the motorway the lovers
Are shadows filling a wood:
Between them the space nothing crosses:
    Foetus in a jar.

Breaking Down

I

The ice-plant thrusts out of the slabs,
And roses, crushed like paper, are sweetest
In ruin. This garden was not
An ordered place for nothing was subject
To your will. Things lived and died
And of their brief flourish you made
No calculation. But the roots pulled up
In rusty sheaves left fingers traced
With iodine; there were black half-moons
Of dirt under your nails. And simply,
As a child explores, the spade you tempered
In that earth made annual discoveries:
The buttercup stem's blue meths-colour
Like a glint of porcelain, the seams
Of coal, or charcoal, thin as razorblades
Peeled from the clay. And you cut nothing,
Watched grass grow tall and the purple
Seed-sheaths fatten and release
Their sticky mist of grain, the cool
Unsweet convolvulus lassoing every shoot.
So boundaries blurred, the poplars
Shed their curious white fleece
And the heavy vines of bryony
Like broken counting-frames
Troubled the eye: an exotic sprawl
Respecting no margin, your challenge
Of abundance to the neighbours' sober lawns.
Majorities of course prefer straight lines.

One day arriving home I found
The unfamiliar whine of saws
Filling the garden, the hedge gleaming
With scores of white amputations,
Its severed wood glossy as a sucked bone.
Two sawyers cursed their blades' rhythm
While a fountain of flies played over them,
Green and blue, the living smoke
Of all the colonies they had disturbed,
The evicted populations of the trees.
And there you stood, observing everything,
Urging that drastic husbandry,
A new bronze switch of sycamore
Humming in your fist, its delicate
Sheath of inner-bark green as a magpie's foot.
I remember that, I remember
A voice cleaned even of desperation;
But an attitude struck, a pose that would last:
The etching of a crisis in your face.

II

A leaping boy with pollen-coloured hair,
That girl whose creaky leg-iron
Looked like the letter H. The teeming past,
Enigma of memory! Your childhood
Was the story I never quite believed,
Its hoard of detail challenging
The present's sparser life.
But thrilling, such talent for swift recall,
The lacquered moments from history's fog.
A children's council meets again
In a clearing of a wood, yellow grass
And the cool baize of moss, a circle
Of foxgloves, tall, wizard-like,
And lichen black as surgical stitch
A sharp seam on the rock. So the dead,
The sick, the mad, the amnesiac,
Those for whom the past has been
The cruellest of times, ally once more
In youth's confederacy; before
They vanish, ghosts in frayed jerseys,
Faces stained with the dust of moths
And dandelion milk. Leaving time on your hands.
Now the hours shoot away
Like seeds from the broom's black pods;
Each day a small, dry detonation,
And the fruit gone.

III

The windows spill their brilliance on the street,
Your neighbours there, the rituals of their lives.
That woman whose eyes are a lizard's
Lidless bulge, the girl with comic limp,
Why single them out? They are as familiar
Here as the rainbow of oil on hot
Asphalt, the hawkbit's yellow crowns.

But the child whose face crumpled in the womb
Is a man now, led carefully by the hand
Through streets where hay and petrol smells
Compete for mastery of the air:
He will be trudging here the next century,
Walking in circles. This place they dump
Their wounded in, pretend it's a different world.

Your youth might know it, and yet not find you.
A thousand souls or so at the head
Of the plain, the slate and spar of cottages
Between pincers of the new estates.
These houses' gypsum sparkles when the light
Is strong, and ash-keys' tropical swatches,
Pendulant green manes of seeds, still brush the ground.

And this the place of all places
That you have understood; made deeper, stranger,
With your life. I've seen you toss some clothes
Into a bag, thrust banknotes crushed

Like sweetpapers into a ragged suit,
Run shouting at a wall that hurls you back.
But we clear up the face-powder, the springy

Balls of tights, parry a truth that one day
Might have pierced. I remember the works
And their orange bricks with the village name
Stamped blackly in each crust. The railway yard
Was full of their huge sprawl, a desert's
Colour, or the ruins of something scarcely built.
Here's your powder like the brickdust on my sleeve.

IV

You forgot your glasses and mackintosh;
In the rush to leave there was only time
For the thought of getting out; the escape:
A ticket, a bag, a room, your place away.
Later, we come after you, a family
That uses all the cadences of hurt
And injustice; that pretends it is betrayed.
Your palms are soiled and wrinkled as banknotes,
I shiver as they fall upon my head.
What aches is love, or duty; the trapped nerve.

St. Chad's is in the Broadway, a road
Of lock-up shops, a tanker like a scarlet chrysalis,
The dark Victorian mortar charcoal-dry.
And still I cannot guess what kind of hope
Had made you knock and walk into this place,
The salty words that met you, the indifference.
Some doors loom fearfully, show no way back:
There might not be a world away from this
Tall shuttered room with its margins of light,
The shadows' long spokes from the window bars.

'Anyone can come in here.' You make it sound
Like a library or public-house. 'They don't care
Who you are or where you're from'.
And the talk goes on, the words of strangers
In a dull, unintelligible burr, the talk
That spins a web around our names.

A radio plays and someone lights the blue cones
Of the gas; we sit on sofas plaiting their leaked straw.
'They're all so good, I share a dormitory.
The men and women queue for the bathroom'.

And then you take a ha'penny from your coat,
Small red coin on your hand like a scab.
It buys exactly nothing and is your loud boast:
'Look at this, this money is all I have' —
Its proud possession a tribal mark.
And look around, you say, for these are all
Your friends, boasters too, showing their nothing
To the world in some preposterous challenge.
And they wait, these few, with terrible patience
For everything they know will not happen.

V

Joan

Joan's face belongs to an immaculate
Corpse: blue coins of mascara
Over each eye-white, cheekbones traced
With powder coarse as ice. She never speaks
But lives behind an image of cool, shocked beauty.
Her summer vest is bright as jeweller's rouge.

Sarge

An army man with face as mobile
As water, his fingers red and splayed.
St. Chad's is a barracks softer than most;
It has the smoke from his plate's pyramid of rice,
The TV screen's cold breast of glass.
He sits with the dogs, hands twisting
Their throats' black silk, and talks
Entirely in stunned expletives
Of the way the Japanese captured his friends,
Then hung microphones in the forest
To broadcast their screams. These histories
Pass unnoticed as the news.

John

Beard a terse silver, plimsolls peeling
Back like sardine tins. He's a postman
And he gasps the litany of farm names,
His cycle skidding down their frozen ruts:
House in the Speckled Land, Enchanter's Rock,
The Hammer's Thunder, House at Iago's Well.
It's a late delivery in those parts,
And the pastures under the gridiron
Of the spruce. He gulps the air, and we hear
The words freeze on his tongue; huge,
Awkward as icecubes, the stammerer's fright.
But the cigarette glows against his mouth
With all the lucidity of breath
He is denied: his twin in smoke, man-high,
The faint companion is writhing at his side,
A spirit that does not choke upon its speech
And has never felt the shackle at the throat.

VI

In this city a reek of malt
The characteristic pungency.
City of breweries and their
Seaweed rankness, the waste
Poured down the river's sluice
In a floe of yellow foam.

District of locked Victorian
Streets silent behind zinc:
Spice baskets green with dill,
Orange with turmeric:
Mr Arakan never closes till ten;
His posters fly, slashing like gullwings.

Tenement of olive brick,
A dormitory with bare plumbing.
The ledges of that bed have known
A hundred like you set to trace
The lost property of their lives.
But eyes squeezed shut can't black us out.

VII

You never hear a word of our advice.
In the city the sky's a low ceiling,
Its light a thumbed glass.
What's to see but the whirlpool of faces?
People don't look at you. They never speak.
There's something ahead they are always hurrying to,
A secret they won't share.

In the car you tell the day's adventures:
The price of coffee and bus journeys,
How you sat at a khaki stall in Social
Security counting cigarette burns
In the carpet. And then that other public room,
Dirty, raucous, smoky with mirrors.
You walked to the counter and gripped its rail.

The homeless gather in there
And the fugitives from home.
Square, uproarious women and their venous
Men; a few, like pinched ascetics, china-white.
You'd never known such shameless company:
A failed solicitor's rape stories
Blossoming out of the gin,

Criminology of the bar-room
And the yellow legends of sex:
Somewhere, in a lane, a body slashed.
And you offer us the details like a child's discoveries,
All the accents of astonishment
Juggling in your voice. The world's like this,
This world. The car points home.

VIII

Everything tastes of something else.
I push the plate away but you
Craving sweetness lick the tiny
Chocolate splinters round with your tongue,
Suck up the pool of smoke-coloured cream.
A cafe by a viaduct, enormous
Breastworks split by long diagonals of shade
Creeping like black moss against the bricks.

Something about your face has changed:
The eyes between their bruises look elsewhere,
And faintly now, but intricate as webs,
The wrinkles start to press into your skin.
Smile, and your cheeks are hollow as spoons,
Glance away and there returns that mark
Of ugly concentration, like purse-strings
Pulling tight within your brow.

We drive down through the valley where
The terracing of shopfronts casts
Parallelograms of light. A long time
Since you looked in these windows, and all
The goods have changed. Digital clocks
Show seconds pass in a shower of green sparks,
The stereo decks are piled up like glass bricks.
Only the river runs traditionally,

Tugging its quilt of iron dust,
While an apprentice in a marble room
Saws at some creature's axles of bone,
The falling meat like hanks of red satin.
The day is full of ceremonies
In which you play no part. Its assault
Comes from colours, faces, words, your own thoughts'
                                        treachery:
Our claim on you is part of its strangeness.

IX

We walk in the garden through corridors
Of sycamore. Music breathes from another
House, a maybug drones in the dusk.
Our kitchen light's clear porcelain
Shows a crusting of burnt moths.

You don't talk now and there are no books;
The great Lives in pillars around your chair
Returned to shelves, the dictionary
A forgotten tool. It's pills we place
Beside your plate, watch their poisons wither you.

The scented-stock is an evening kindled,
Sweetly burning gum. Green nets of
Convolvulus rustle in the dark, tightening
Like webs around their flower-prey.
A wasp spins mummified in silken bonds.

We're all pinned here, the prison's in our heads;
Backyard dogs chained to a wall
By our fear and our history. So when you escape
We have to bring you home, knowing no other place.
It's what you see, and seek, that terrifies.

X

Latin's the fit language for the stars,
Their bright sterility. You named
The constellations as they swung
Over our heads, fuzzy balls of
Galaxies pulsing in a glass,
The Milky Way's fine spiderweb.

It's only now we understand.
You have been looking away from here
For a long time, gently discarding
Us from your mind. You're breaking out,
Becoming what you always were.
And still at times it feels like a betrayal.

XI

You threw the tablets in the toilet bowl:
Orange, red and black their slow suspensions
In water, like the fruit clusters
Of the wayfaring tree, its bitter lozenges.

The whole house is a medicine-cabinet.
About the rooms the bottles lie with tops
You cannot unscrew, barbiturates
Like bryony's livid grapes, and the small
Metallic rattle of some forgotten dose
Seeds in a pod. Their coloured grains
Are pollen that escapes a cracked capsule.

We hang stones on your limbs, parch your lips,
Tie you to a chair and drain the well
Of your mind, fill your mouth with ashes
And your body with dead flowers,
Thrust the scissors' steel against the stems of your hair.

There's a cloud in your eye but no protest.
Every step is now
A particular greeting of the dust. Such care.
And words, being migratory,
Have all gone.
These pills work.

XII

A redbrick mansion in its own estate
Of fields and darker shrubberies
Where statues lean amongst the shadows'
Camouflage. A place to change ideas.
That woman, rouged and striking
As an artificial flower, the toothless
Men who mulch their food — their entry
Is made effortless into this
Closed order, secret society.

The Hospital   *To Pose*

XIII

They walk and cup the precious cigarettes,
Pace the corridors and sun-flooded ward,
Smoking, stubbing, relighting the butts,
Look comic, vacant, desperate and bored.

I want to give him a lovebite, the red-
Head says, eyes polished like bits of quartz;
In my arms tonight not in my thoughts,
I want to have him lying in my bed.

On the ceiling the black stalactite
Of someone's meal, the deep tan of the smoke
An older stain. Out of here in a week
If I wanted, they say; I could come tonight,

Pack a suitcase and walk over the hill,
Feel the frost sting like a hypodermic,
Hear the river running when the air is still.
Or less than a week: perhaps less than a week.

I want to take my man to the ward, that's all,
I want to kiss his mouth until it hurts,
Or less than a week, past the cattle
Grazing in Cae Morfa, breath pouring like spurts

Of milk. I know, I've pulled their tits,
Their eyelashes like beautiful moss, so womanly,
His body next to mine a few minutes,
So silent, patient, a hot side touching me.

XIV

We would go there for fossils, the cliffsides
Rich with those shadows of life, ammonites
Curled tight as catherine-wheels, the grey bodies
Of rockpool creatures chalk-marks on a slate.
Our chisels freed them from the steep limestone.

Now a taxi takes you to that quiet place
Through a resort still off-season; a child
Plays in a farm beili, dun farrow and
A green silo the afternoon's landmarks.
Such things might stop the heart, or mean nothing.

The weather clear, but you in overcoat
And boots; there's still a sinew in the wind
And surf is booming at the mouths of caves,
The moraines of coloured plastics on the shore
And all the bleached hillocks of sea-litter.

'A good day for a walk', he says, 'have fun',
And spins the red Cortina through the lanes.
And then there is only you and the great
Game of forgetting, an act of concentration
Meant to dissolve a life. Like blowing a sparrow's

Egg perhaps, dark, still, and rough as ice
That perfect thing, a scribble on its shell.
So you move against the slow current
And your calves ache as the next wave slaps
Like some cold green fern over your coat,

And then you are in the undergrowth
As the water opens around you huge
Colourless flowers with a choking scent,
A noose of vines that plucks you from your feet.
Soon the roots of the forest are pressed against your
                                                    mouth.

Tight as an ammonite you lie curled
In the white stone of the bed. A face of chalk,
And salt-stiff hair that brushes can't untie,
Arranged upon the sheet. Do fossils dream?
Tomorrow when you wake we'll talk and talk.

Born in 1942, Robert Minhinnick has lived in Maesteg and the village of Pen-y-Fai in Mid Glamorgan. He has now settled with his wife and small daughter in Porthcawl, and works as the manager of an environmental project on the Glamorgan Heritage Coast. **The Dinosaur Park** is his fourth collection of poems and in many ways is a departure from his previous work. Of his last book, **Life Sentences**, the critics wrote:

'the outstanding poet of his generation in Britain.'
— *Outposts*

'there is so much to praise, so much excellence to delight in.' — *Poetry Wales*